Blossoms of Hope

Other Titles by Justin Farley

Poetry

- A Voice in the Wilderness
  - A Chapbook of Poems About God
- Nature's Bounty
  - A Chapbook of Poems About Nature
- Thorns of Love
  - Sad Love Poems
- Frozen Rivers
  - Poems About Winter and Mental Illness

Blossoms of Hope

Justin Farley

Inkspiration Books

Acknowledgement to The Wee Sparrow Press where *Faithful Fishing* and *Of Sea and Shore* first appeared in altered form in "Hope is a Group Project: A Poetry Anthology".

Birdsong first appeared in the collection, "Nature's Bounty: A Chapbook of Poems About Nature".

For my family who have never given up on me despite my struggles, and for the redemptive power of hope-- the Light in the Darkness.

A Note on the Context of These Poems

"Blossoms of Hope" is the second book of a tetralogy--a book for each season of the year. Half of each book contains poems about nature pertaining to that season and half about a mental illness / mental health topic that I feel the season personifies.

The first book in this series, "Frozen Winters", focused on both the bleakness and beauty of nature during winter. For the mental illness section, the theme centered around depression, coinciding with the dull and dead of the season.

This collection contains two sections that alternate every poem: *Blossoms of the Mind* are mainly hopeful poems about dealing with mental illness and the hardships of life; *Blossoms of Life* are poems that celebrate the growth and hope of spring. They center around the birth of new life in nature and the joy that comes from the end of winter.

I've struggled with mental illness for most of my life and want to bring awareness to a struggle that's still widely misunderstood and to give a voice to those bravely fighting their battle in silence. These poems were written from real experiences in the trenches of life and will hopefully bring some light into your own.

Hope has been my constant companion. Without it, I wouldn't be able to function. Mental illness is challenging and downright miserable some days. To deny that is to deny the condition itself. But I've also discovered a beautiful life even in the midst of the struggle. It's not always easy, but it's always worth it.

I don't know what you're going through, but you're not alone. My hope with this collection (and series) is that by sharing some of my dark places my readers might find solidarity in their struggle and some hope in my small victories.

I'm not cured and don't want to paint a picture of a life

that's all put together. I don't have all the answers but have found a way to wake up every day with gratitude and some semblance of contentment even though many of my days are very difficult. If you're needing help, please reach out to a professional.

My current plan is to do summer next which will center around mania--summer being the brightest and most energetic season of the year. The series will close with a fall collection that will revolve around anxiety, since fall is seen as the beginning of the end of the year. Endings often coincide with apprehension for the future, the unknowns associated with death, and the end of comfortable and familiar relationships and experiences.

Thank you for joining me on my journey!

With Love,

Justin Farley

CONTENTS

Blossoms of the Mind

Blossoms of Life

Stitching Pain

I'm taking my pain

and sewing it into a quilt

stitched with wisdom and blessing.

I know it will do nothing

to eradicate the source of your suffering

or the bitter chill of this world,

but perhaps it will bring you

some comfort knowing

you aren't alone in your sorrows.

Perhaps it will provide some warmth

and something to curl up under

when the winds of your winter begin to blow.

Songs of Spring

The robins are out chirping,

and the cardinals have resumed their singing.

They've reemerged from the bushes and brush

used for cover from the harsh wind

these past few winter months.

They come bearing joy.

They come carrying the hope

that I can cope and wait out this last cold front.

For spring is just around the corner.

Each day gets warmer,

and the sun hangs in the sky

a minute or two longer.

Even those damn sparrows

that fly in flocks of five hundred,

that fight and jabber throughout the day,

and take dirt baths in the craters

of a driveway slowly being returned to nature

4

bring a smile to my face

and build a nest of laughter in my belly

even knowing

this temporary ceasefire won't last--

by the end of summer

there will be dozens of reasons

to despise them, to wish their deaths.

But for now, we share the morning

as friends, both delighting

that at long last,

winter's grasp

is slowly slipping away.

Faithful Fishing

Blossoms of the Mind

Joy can be tasted

even in the depths of suffering

by savoring the fruits of hope.

Each sunrise erases yesterday's demise

and evokes the grace to cope

with the rapid-fire of endless trials

that test the strength of faith

like a hooked salmon fiercely fighting,

desperately trying to drag you downstream--

yanked by the current of self-pity,

pulling you into the depths of depression

where life is dammed.

But joy and hope continue reeling,

continue pulling in and fighting against

the downcast spirit that simply

wants to be released

and sink like a stone beneath the water

to lie lifeless on the floor of life.

I've tasted the fruits of hope

not because my suffering has ceased

but because I keep reeling in

this shadow part of myself

and equip my line with a steel leader of faith

that can never be broken.

Blossoms of Hope

Blossoms of Life

Bees are back pollinating flowers.

Fawns are taking their first wobbly steps.

Darkness arrives later each evening.

Tadpoles swim in the ponds' shallow depths.

Birds are busy flitting through forests,

chirping and beginning to build nests.

Grass is growing; flowers are blooming.

Rebirth has replaced the stench of death.

Nature sends her prudent reminders

through the fragrance of the blossoms' breath--

when all signs point to endless winter,

hopeful seeds plan for spring nonetheless.

Resilience

Remember me as resilient.

Let my epitaph not read

mighty, fearless, or even a man of peace--

for I live a life of war,

constantly engaged in battle

with my inner demons.

But let the stone cry out

I never gave up

through the trials of Job.

Let it record

I failed a thousand times over

yet never allowed

defeat to define me.

But let the engraved inscription

credit hope, grace, and mercy

as the arms that carried me.

Resiliency rarely appears

as an immovable and nearly invincible force

like a massive boulder upon a beach.

I'm more like a tall oak tree

who's withstood storm after storm,

who keeps from breaking by bending

under the strain of the fierce winds of life.

I have an expiration date when

my trunk will finally split

under the angry gust of a tornado

or a sudden strike of lightning,

but you'll have to rip me up by the roots

if you want me gone

because I'll carry on damaged,

doing my best to stand tall though broken.

Remember me as resilient.

Seasons of Winter

Blossoms of Life

The ice is melting,

thawing away from the land,

flowing back into the hands

of its maker.

Nature's enchantment shatters

with a single kiss from spring

whose lips cling to the warmth

of renewal, rebirth, and reawakening.

With each pile of snow

that dissolves, my heart beats

in rhythm with hope,

sledding down slopes of solace,

taking comfort in the possibility to cope

with my own season of winter.

Great Expectations

Blossoms of the Mind

Joy can seize us

in the lowliest of places,

perhaps even easier

than in the loftiest ones.

Humble eyes are open wider

than those of great expectation,

those muted of exultation

and closed to the blessings

that abound in the ordinary;

its commonness makes it no less miraculous.

It's easy to see the glory

of God when you step out

of a cave flooded with darkness.

Far harder blind, perched upon

an idolatrous mountaintop of our own making.

Great expectations can't bring joy

when they're contingent on the false hope

that joy can be gained

from obtaining anything of worldly worth.

14

Happiness is fleeting,

but joy remains though the seasons change--

in both the harsh, winter cold

and the warm, summer sun.

A joyful heart shoots for the stars

but is content if the Universe wills

for it to remain on Earth.

Migrating

A flock of ducks fly overhead,

their flapping wings

illuminated by the warm glow of dawn.

They head north into new waters

now that winter is thawing

from the lakes, ponds, and rivers.

We've convinced ourselves that a permanent home

is the ultimate sign of achievement and freedom.

But watching you fly across the morning sky

gives me plenty of reason to doubt,

wondering if it's not actually a prison.

For you are free to pursue

whatever adventure calls to you

and have seen and swam in diverse waters,

while I still float in this tepid pool

bound by fixed borders.

Sowing

Blossoms of the Mind

To harvest, you must first sow,

or you'll end up in a fall

with nothing to show for all

the time that's passed except

acres of fields covered with weeds,

regretting doing nothing with the seeds

you held in spring.

Change comes slowly,

rarely overnight.

Take delight in cultivating

your corner of beauty in the world.

Never allow your crop to be ravaged by crows of woe.

For no other garden will ever offer the world

the unique nutrients you grow.

So sow.

Sow what you know.

Sow the seeds that are undeniably you.

Sow the seeds that make you want

to take root and reach up to drink the sun.

But whatever you do,

sow.

Birdsong

The birds of morning take their places

upon the stage of life's amphitheater

where their voices have remained mute for months.

But today, they rise in joyful chorus,

belting out hymns of healing.

Isn't it remarkable how a giant-sized footprint

can be left upon the soul by such a small animal

and lift a heavy heart higher

than pharmaceutical cocktails and cognitive endeavors

by a voice that sweeps the soot from the soul's chimney

with only chirps in rhythmic time

and playful ruffles of feathers?

Somewhere, subconsciously, we believe

these fragile, feathered fairies are the gatekeepers of spring

and have enough magic in their beaks

to end this bleak, cursed winter.

Their songs are beautiful incantations,

awakening nature from her hibernation

and inviting all who hear their music back to life.

Walk On

Blossoms of the Mind

If the road stretches you,

walk on.

Sprint, stumble, or crawl

but walk on.

Don't look for the exit signs,

the mile markers, rest stops, or places to lodge.

Fix your focus on the road ahead

instead of the billboards advertising ease.

Hold your destination firmly in your hands

or else it'll slip through your fingers

and sift to the ground like sand.

When you're lonely out on the journey,

make perseverance and patience your best friends.

Ignore the potholes and the unevenness of the road,

and no matter if all the traffic clears out by night fall,

walk on.

.

Don't be surprised when it rains; weather's destined to change.

When it threatens to destroy you, pull out positivity,

make it a shield, and carry it like an umbrella.

No one lives in the comfort of summer all year long.

Your journey may have begun under the warmth of the sun

but fall's coming and with it a chilly breeze,

warning you of the coming winter

with temperatures guaranteed to knock you to your knees.

There will be days when an inch is all your spirit can handle

and others where you'll float above the weight of gravity,

flying without getting tired.

But don't be distracted by distances;

even the weakest minds can manage miles

when walking on smooth, flat planes.

Worry about suiting up and showing up

when misery is calling your name.

Put one foot in front of the other and carry on

no matter what anyone tells you--

not even that voice living in your head

repeating the harmful words others have said

and is always worrying about what's ahead.

Your destination always lies on the other side of today,

so no matter what comes your way,

walk on.

Therapy Session

Blossoms of Life

I checked into therapy

and found the waiting room empty.

The silence soothed my wounds.

No distractions. No social interactions.

Nothing but towering waves of peace

washing over and carrying out to sea

the worries of my mind

like waters lapping upon a beach.

Ah, the doctor is ready to see me.

I strip my soul naked,

stand in awe observing God's creation,

and bathe in the stream

of heaven's glorious light.

At the end of my session,

I thank the mighty oak,

the flowing river,

the grazing deer,

the squawking jay,

and the playful squirrel

for all of their wisdom.

I asked Mother Nature

what I owed her.

No charge.

The Heavy Fog of the Mind

Blossoms of the Mind

Yesterday's heavy fog of depressive mist
has dissipated, and I can finally see clearly.
That dark, alien force in my mind has gone
and taken with it the hollow emptiness of apathy.

Light has reappeared at the tunnel's end,
and hope rises again from the ashes of the dead.
The crushing weight of these covers has been lifted;
I'm able to break through the bonds that held me in bed.

Like the sky, my mood can change daily
as dramatic as day morphs into night.
Today can find me submerged in a jet-black sea;
tomorrow blinded by the intensity of piercing light.

But I won't fret over tomorrow's grief
when the weather today is quite fine.
Yesterday's heavy fog of depressive mist has dissipated,
and joyful bliss has reemerged in my mind.

Recharging

Green shoots break through

leaves flushed of color

and piled across the forest floor;

life pushes aside the ash

of last year's trash to make room for the new.

The echoes of voices and chirps

are becoming dampened

by the emerging leaves

covering the trees' naked limbs.

The rivers and streams have begun

sending out their invitations to feet

as their icy waters

are warmed by the spring sun.

As nature lifts her veil

of darkness and death,

the invigorating energy of new life

surges through the air

across invisible power lines

that all living cells

feel and plug into,

recharging after being drained dead

by the consuming cold of winter.

No Quarter

Blossoms of the Mind

If I look, I'll find 1000s of complaints,

but I've resolved to give no quarter to grumbles

when I've been so blessed with gifts that have tumbled

down from Heaven like manna.

If I find my vision

dull, dark, and gray

it's because I've chosen to stay

blind to how lucky I truly am.

Of course there's darkness.

But there's also an abundance of light

available when we keep our sight

fixed on our graces and gratitude.

Dark clouds, let the wind blow you on by.

I'll no longer grant you quarter.

My attitude is back in order;

my storehouse is far too full to harbor complaint.

Morning Star

Blossoms of Life

Morning star, oh, how faithful you are

to lead me across the sea of night.

In the midst of my toughest fight,

hope is never far--

for I can look up and find strength in your light.

Morning star, won't you shine?

Won't you remind me dawn is starting to rise?

She is yawning, calling for the night's demise.

Shine, lift up this heavy heart of mine.

For hope relies on your presence in the skies.

I Will Hear the Robin Sing

Blossoms of the Mind

I blasted through the bedrock of night,

plugged my ears as I lit the fuse that coiled

like a snake towards TNT packed tight with hope.

I chipped away at the darkness

that surrounded me like a miner in a shaft,

searching for something of substance

in this hungry cavern of emptiness

that's swallowed me deep within its pitch-black bowels

where the air hangs thick in damp sheets

like wet laundry on a clothesline in the backyard.

But here, there's no external heat source

to dry you out; the only fire you can warm yourself by

is the internal flame of resistance

and the belief that there's a reason,

a purpose for your existence

higher and deeper than that of a mangy, starving animal

that rambles throughout the night,

moving just to fend off the cold and the fear.

But no matter how alone I feel,

I know my story doesn't end here.

One day, morning will finally lift this veil of suffering.

Then, this thick cloud of darkness will depart

and take away the horrors my cruel thoughts often bring.

There will be an end to this long, dark night;

I will live to hear the robin sing!

Metamorphosis

It inched along the earth
crunching, munching on misfortune
until pain wrapped itself like a cocoon
around the outside of a hardened heart.

Drowning, surely dying in the dark,
only to emerge from the womb
reborn from a tomb of self-inflicted wounds--
transformed by Divinity's spark.

With wings of vibrant color
carrying the evidence of change,
arrayed like a roadmap
dotted with places been and places going.

Flapping with the wings of grace,
carried by a breeze of blessing.
A chrysalis replaced,
made anew by the Spirit's pressing.

The Road to Avalon

Blossoms of the Mind

She bid adieu to the life she knew
and walked away without hesitation.
For she was stuck in her situation
and needed a way out to start anew.

The pain of yesterday lingered longer
than the girl could have ever imagined
but being forced to face and slay dragons
grew her confidence and made her stronger.

And she still remembered her childhood fears,
but they were buried under resolved will
to keep moving forward despite the chill
memory brings when it swiftly appears.

The road to Avalon is paved with pain--
sometimes unfair but with purpose and goal.
For to walk it you must transform your soul,
and there your true self is found and obtained.

The Pecking Order of Life

I watch a horde of sparrows

peck and claw, nose-dive and scratch

one of their own to death.

The poor victim tries to beat back the blows,

but it's engaged in an unfair fight

with wings beating the life

out of its small body by the bullies

surrounding its delicate frame.

I feel like a teacher

watching chaos unfold on the playground

but know I'm incapable

of breaking up this death sentence;

they will follow

this poor fellow to its grave,

and I can't fly to its rescue.

At last, its motionless body

rests upon the grass.

It's not nature

but the memory of Eden

we flee to in order to escape

the evils of humanity.

Nature is merely a reflection

of her former self.

Her trees are just as likely

to strangle you as hug you.

She's not some oasis

in the middle of this desert of life.

Sure, she's dazzling and beautiful

but can be an ugly, fickle bitch

filled with sin just like all the rest of us.

Joyful Jitters

Blossoms of the Mind

What beauty there is,

what hope there is

in the reemergence of the sun's rays

and the thawing of ice and snow.

But as one affliction flees the mind

a familiar foe returns through

its open door and grows.

As energy and warmth

are reabsorbed into the body,

so too comes an edginess,

a chaotic ball of fiery zest rolling in the brain

that can set the mind ablaze

with mania or panic without warning

and send cortisol levels soaring once again.

It would be so much easier

to anchor thoughts to the present moment

with the unbreakable, iron trappings

of heavy ball-and-chain!

But knowing this menacing enemy is marching

diminishes joy and sends anticipatory fear rushing,

flooding the channels of the brain.

Snowing in April

Blossoms of Life

How am I expected to control

the unpredictable fluctuations of my mood

if you are just as bipolar as me?

The average temperature for this time of year

is damn near seventy,

but I wake to find my yard covered with snow.

I've grown so tired of this cold.

I need some heat radiating in my life

to awaken these bones from hibernation

and ignite this dull, dry mind--

get it buzzing like the bees

I've yet to see.

Old Man Winter,

I know you're weary.

It's far time you lean back in your recliner,

prop up your feet,

and rest those frost-laced eyes.

It's time you sleep so spring can arise.

Of Sea and Shore

Blossoms of the Mind

Hope is a shore
rising to meet an endless sea.
A beach that turns back
the tides of misery.

And though the waves
continue to crash upon the shore,
you're no longer thrashing,
treading water anymore.

Like shells that line
the edges of the sea,
the heart will forever hold
echoes of past misery.

But with feet firmly planted
upon the sand of hope's shore,
the heart begins sowing gratitude,
grateful it's not drowning anymore.

A Ballad of a Midwestern Farmer in Spring

Blossoms of Life

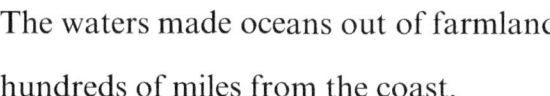

The river rose and crested

over its banks.

Spilled out of the forests

and flooded the fields

like a glass of water knocked over.

The waters made oceans out of farmland

hundreds of miles from the coast.

Ducks swam in seas

floored with corn and soybeans.

And the farmer looked on,

thankful for the rich nutrition

from the silt deposits of the rivers and streams,

hopeful for a plentiful harvest,

but praying the sky

clears up before

a blessing turns into a curse.

A Vault of Darkness

Blossoms of the Mind

When does this tunnel of blinding darkness

run out of shadows to seal off my days?

When does this gloom ridden haze

hanging over my head like a heavy fog

stop weighing my mind down and dissipate?

My spirit yearns for the rejuvenating rains of spring

like a parched throat craves water in desert heat.

I sit at my table and find a stale, rotten feast

that consists of nothing but black

crumpets of emptiness to eat.

But this force of antimatter

underestimates the beating in my breast

and fails to detect the fight I have left

in the deepest recesses of my soul.

I will bear my sentence

in this vault of darkness

until my mind claws and climbs

its way out of this deep, dark hole.

Growing Daffodils

Blossoms of Life

Buds of daffodils

begin opening their eyes,

roused by April's warmth.

Like miniature suns,

constellations of color

explode from petals.

Rays of hope appear

to a world plagued by darkness

and starving for light.

Running

Can I get a cup of wine

to drown the time,

to float away from

this heavy heart of mine?

Or perhaps a fast car

that'll dash me far

away from these expired dreams--

a night now void of stars?

Maybe a boat to sail these seas,

waters that swallow me with ease

each time the tide of my mood

drags me out to thrash about with no reprieve?

But I suppose that won't do

because there's no way to bid adieu

to my mind who follows me

no matter where I run to.

I can't conspire to flee

when my jailer is me.

I only get to taste freedom

by working on myself daily.

Nature's Chord

Blossoms of Life

The fluttering of a thousand wings fill the sky--

blackbirds and geese fly to unknown destinations.

The cool dew of morning runs

down blades of grass.

Fog hovers beneath the trees,

and the sun begins to peak out over the horizon.

All is silent, all is still

until at all once

trumpets blare from tiny beaks,

announcing the break of day.

There's no greater mystery for those who choose

to open their eyes and ears to it.

There's no way to gaze upon the transformation

and not be stunned in stupefied wonder.

For He has written the tune

upon each and every heart,

so that all may recognize His glory

when nature's chord is strummed.

Growing Pains

Why are these dreams that stretch out

across my heart's field of desire

and glisten like droplets of dew

sparkling on the morning grass

so hard to attain,

so hard to lasso

and pull close to reality?

I know what I need lies just beyond the forest

and through this grove of trees.

It's a burden being able to see where the path leads

but being unable to bring myself to action.

So often I'm fixated on distractions

that pull me off-course and send me down rabbit holes

instead of moving me towards goals and destinations.

Carrying around bags of frustration drives a person mad,

grueling under their weight day after day,

counting the minutes, certain there's another way.

But the Way is an untrodden path--

a trip packed for but never taken--

and hope begins dimming like light from a flickering bulb

until it burns out at its expiration.

There's a demon inside of me

who scoffs at dreams, is content to let life pass me by,

tramples on schedules,

curses meaningful causes,

and who seems unable to be controlled.

Impish claws dig into my hands and seize me

each time I reach out to grasp my goals.

I now know the paved road to success doesn't exist.

You must venture through the dense forest,

fight through the thicket,

and thrash through the sticks.

To journey with intention is no vacation,

and the mess inside me--

always attempting to misguide me--is no easy fix.

But the trail to nowhere is covered by countless footprints

and paved with the trampled dreams

others have left behind.

In the silent moments when all the noise

of obligation and diversions cease, wisdom speaks.

I hear, but for a reason I've yet to understand,

I refuse to listen.

Waning Crescent Moon

Blossoms of Life

A beautiful slice of heaven

hangs in the night.

A sliver of hope--

a sliver of light--

that refuses to surrender

to the surrounding darkness.

Down to its last stand

before it's inevitably

swallowed by shadow.

But from each death, new light is born,

streaming forth from the new moon's passing.

Each cycle, the waning crescent

rises and fights once more

despite its failed attempts

billions of times before

and its innumerable defeats to come.

Its tenacity is a beautiful beacon

for all who take the time

to gaze upon its light--

a symbol for those trapped in the night

who are tempted to quit shinning

in the midst of flooding darkness.

Thank you!

Thank you, dear reader, for taking the time to read my work! I hope my words have touched you. Indie writers rely on people like you to review their work. I'd greatly appreciate your feedback.

Please subscribe to my newsletter for monthly updates of new content, news related to book releases / current projects, and special offers through the link in my Instagram bio @justinfarleypoet or on my blog @alongthebarrenroad.com/links

If you enjoyed this collection, you may also be interested in the first book in this series, "Frozen Rivers", or my three other collections ("A Voice in the Wilderness", "Nature's Bounty", and "Thorns of Love").

Acknowledgements

Mental illness takes a toll not only on people suffering from the illness but also on the people that love them. Living with me isn't always easy. A giant thank you to my patient, loving wife and my family for their unconditional love.

I'm also grateful for hope. I'm grateful for faith. I'm grateful that God has gifted me with the ability to find contentment in a life that is heavily impacted by mental illness. There's a whole lot of days that are downright miserable, but by grace, I very rarely fall into a mindset overwhelmed by hopelessness. And I'm grateful for the plasticity of the human mind--that we are able change, to sow, and to grow new life.

About the Author

Justin Farley is a poet, writer, and songwriter living in Indianapolis, IN. His writing has been published in numerous journals and typically centers around nature, spirituality, and mental health.

He blogs at www.alongthebarrenroad.com. Follow him on Instagram @justinfarleypoet. Join his newsletter for updates and promotions @alongthebarrenroad.com/links

Printed in Great Britain
by Amazon